Jean Andrews was born and grew up in the West of Ireland. A poet and translator of poetry, she teaches at the Department of Spanish, Portuguese and Latin American Studies at the University of Nottingham, UK.

While the Men Are Dying
by Carmen Conde

Translated by Jean Andrews

Published 2013 by arima publishing

www.arimapublishing.com

ISBN 978 1 84549 586 2

© Jean Andrews 2013

Printed and bound in the United Kingdom

arima publishing
ASK House, Northgate Avenue
Bury St Edmunds, Suffolk IP32 6BB
t: (+44) 01284 700321

www.arimapublishing.com

Acknowledgements

I am grateful to the Patronato Carmen Conde-Antonio Oliver Belmás, Cartagena, Spain, and its deputy chair, María del Rosario Montero Rodríguez, for permission to publish these translations. I would also like to acknowledge the kind assistance of Caridad Fernández Hernández, librarian-technician at the Patronato.

The cover photograph of Carmen Conde in Jaén (Andalusia) in July 1937 is reproduced by kind permission of the Patronato.

Contents

Introduction

Carmen Conde (1907-1996) is one of the most prolific Spanish writers of the twentieth century. Primarily a poet, she also produced children's literature, drama and fiction, and was the first woman in modern times to be elected to the Spanish Royal Academy of Letters, in 1978.

In the early 1930s, under the socialist Second Republic, she was heavily involved in government-sponsored adult education initiatives, the most significant of which was the Universidad Popular de Cartagena (People's University of Cartagena) which she set up in collaboration with her husband, the poet Antonio Oliver Belmás. In line with government policy on mass literacy and universal access to culture, the mission of this institution was to bring education and a range of cultural production to the urban working classes.[1] During the Civil War, while her husband was engaged in propaganda work as a posts and telegraphs official for government radio at military postings throughout Andalusia, Conde worked sporadically in primary education, pursued a degree course at the University of Valencia and published newspaper articles in support of the government, not all of which were entirely supportive of government policy. After the war, she and her husband, in contrast to the vast majority of the left-wing cultural elite, chose to remain in Spain. While, much later in life she reported this decision as a thoroughly patriotic one guided largely by her husband's sense that it was their duty to remain and not consign the country wholesale to the Nationalists, she herself, by then, also had another loyalty to consider.

She married Antonio Oliver in 1931 but only two years later the birth of a still-born daughter put an end not just to any hopes of a

---

[1] See José Luis Ferris, *Carmen Conde: Vida, pasión y verso de una escritora olvidada* (Madrid: Temas de Hoy, 2007), pp. 319-323.

much-longed for child, but also to the marriage itself in all but name. In February 1936, she met and began a fifty-year relationship with Amanda Junquera, who was married to Cayetano Alcázar, a politically conservative history professor at the University of Murcia who would become Director-General of Universities under the Franco regime. When Conde went into hiding at the end of the Civil War, the beginning of April 1939, it was Junquera's family who hid her in their flat in Madrid for a year until she and Junquera moved to the village of Santo Domingo del Escorial near Madrid. They remained there for another year and then returned to the capital. Conde appeared before a number of government tribunals accused of crimes against the state, before finally having her case dismissed owing to lack of evidence in April 1944.[2] Her husband was arrested in Murcia and sentenced to a long term of imprisonment from which he was released after a short period of incarceration, due to the influence of his brother, a staunch Nationalist. After that, he lived in seclusion in his sister's house in Murcia before finally being reunited with Conde in Madrid in 1945. By then, his health, never robust, had been seriously affected by the privations he experienced at the hands of his brother-in-law, who, even though he had suffered all his life from a congenital heart condition, put him to work on building sites. Given Junquera's husband's position and Oliver's health, there was no question but that Conde, Belmás and her mother would conventionally set up house together when it became possible to do so, in 1945. At the same time, as the forties progressed, Alcázar did his utmost to help Conde and Oliver as they attempted to remake their professional lives.

The Nationalist victory had effectively rendered Conde and Oliver unemployable. In the early years of the Franco Dictatorship they had been obliged to eke out what living they could penning various types of popular literature under a series of pseudonyms. However, while at his death in 1968, Oliver was a much less well-known poet than his wife, he had become a respected literary critic and historian of twentieth-century Murcian art. For her part, Conde had quietly found work, with Alcázar's assistance, as a librarian and editor at the Complutense University in Madrid and

---

[2] Ferris, pp. 513-528.

8

published poetry discreetly under her own name from the mid-forties onwards. After Oliver's death, Conde and Junquera merged their households, Alcázar having predeceased him in 1958. They remained together until the end of Junquera's life, in 1986. She was a victim of Alzheimer's Disease, a fate that also befell Conde who outlived her for a decade, the last third of which was utterly clouded by her illness.

Throughout her life, Carmen Conde's friendships and loyalties spanned every pertinent divide. Under the Second Republic she was known to defend political conservatives who suffered intimidation by leftists. Under the Dictatorship these same friends sheltered and assisted her, a situation which left her open, later in life, to accusations of hypocrisy and political perfidy. She adhered to her innate Catholic spirituality in the thirties, even as Spain became polarised between atheist and virulently anti-clerical elements in the left and the fascist-leaning, ultra-Catholic right. Though far from orthodox in either lifestyle or beliefs, she doughtily defended church property and the clergy when they came under attack from more incendiary elements within the Republic before and during the war. She took financial responsibility for her husband, cared for him in his bouts of illness and ensured, after his death, that his literary legacy would endure by editing his complete works for publication in 1971.[3] She remained on very amiable terms with Caytano Alcázar, even writing an elegy for him on his death.[4] She was a fearless, headstrong, often difficult but extremely big-hearted individual and she lived a commensurately contrary life. Very early in that life, in 1937, she began *Mientras los hombres mueren* (While The Men Are Dying), a collection of prose poems written in the midst of enemy bombardment of the civilian population of Valencia. She was barely thirty years old.

---

[3] Antonio Oliver Belmás, *Obras completas de Antonio Oliver (1923-1965)* (Madrid: Biblioteca Nueva, 1971).
[4] 'Requiem por Cayetano', dated 19th September 1958, in *Carmen Conde: Antología Poética*, Ed., Francisco Javier Diez de Revenga (Madrid: Biblioteca Nueva, 2007), pp. 162-165.

Brocal (Parapet) and *Júbilos* (Jubliation), her first collections, appeared respectively in 1929 and 1934.[5] At this formative stage in her career, and under the tutelage of Oliver, she had decided to specialise in prose poetry, a notoriously difficult minority-intrest genre, but one which enjoyed a vogue in Spain, largely due to the success of her mentor, the Nobel-prize winner, Juan Ramón Jiménez' two collections of prose poetry, *Platero y yo* (Platero and I, 1914) and *Diario de un poeta reciencasado* (Diary of a Newly-Married Poet, 1916). These early collections were, at least on the surface, lyrical and accessible meditations on young love (*Brocal*) and childhood (*Júbilos*). *Mientras los hombres mueren*, her third prose collection, was not only immeasurably darker in tone and concept, it was also modernist in the complex expression of the individual poems and the architecture of the two poem sequences: *Mientras los hombres mueren* itself and 'A los niños muertos en la guerra' (To the Children Killed in the War). Perhaps only such fragmented density would do.

While the Men Are Dying was, it goes without saying, unpublishable in Spain in the first period of the Dictatorship. Instead, it first saw the light of day in Italy, in 1953, in an edition championed by Conde's friend, the academic Juana Granados who published a parallel text edition (with her own translations into Italian) of a large selection of Conde's poetry in the same year.[6] With the gradual relaxation of censorship which finally came in the sixties, it was possible for Emilio Miró to include *Mientras los hombres mueren* in his anthology of Conde's work, *Obra poética* (Poetry), in 1967, though understandably without much fanfare.[7] Conde herself included *Mientras los hombres mueren* in the first volume of her autobiography, *Por el camino, viendo sus orillas* (Along the Road, Looking at its Verges), in 1986, and, as if to close a circle, it fell to Emilio Miró, as editor of the definitive *Obra completa* (Complete Work), published in the centenary year of her

[5] *Brocal* (Madrid: La Lectura, 1929); *Júbilos* (Murcia: Sudeste, 1934).

[6] *Mientras los hombres mueren* (Milan: Cisalpino, 1953); *Carmen Conde: Poesie*, ed. Juana Granados (Milan: Cisalpino, 1953).

[7] Emilio Miró, ed. *Obra poética de Carmen Conde (1929-1966)* (Madrid: Biblioteca Nueva, 1967; 2nd ed, 1979), pp. 185-215.

birth, 2007, to oversee its reappearance in print in a new century.[8] It has been, up to now, one of the least known elements of her considerable oeuvre: because of its difficulty; because it is written in what has been for several decades an unfashionable genre; chiefly, perhaps, because it was not published at the time of its writing, when it might have caught the attention of the reading public. It remains the most considerable poetic testimony by a woman to emerge from the Civil War in Spain and one of the first texts, if not the first, in a major Western European literature to attempt to give voice to the sufferings of women and children, non-combatants, subjected for the first time to the carpet bombing of civilian populations as a tactic of war.

This collection does not, however, stand alone in the nineteen thirties and forties as a literary work of serious political involvement by a woman poet. It is contemporaneous with other collections of poetry by women on war or the effects of political turmoil, some world-renowned such as the Ukrainian Anna Akhmatova's Russian-language *Requiem* which deals with the terrible consequences of the purges and five-year plans of the Soviet regime in the years before the cataclysm of the Second World War. It was composed in 1935-40 and circulated clandestinely for decades before being formally published in 1968. In the English language, women's response to the Second World War is perhaps most clearly represented in the work of the primitive/modernist, Welsh poet, Lynette Roberts. In recognition of this, her *Gods with Stainless Ears* (1951) was re-issued in a new collected edition by Patrick McGuinness in 2005.[9]

Her take on the utter futility of war from the perspective of her isolated community, Llanybri, in rural Carmarthenshire, and her own situation as a wife whose husband is away at war, is encapsulated thus:

Overseas battling in circles of lust:

---

[8] Carmen Conde, *Por el camino, viendo sus orillas*, 3 vols. (Barcelona: Plaza y Janés, 1986), I, pp. 165-191; *Carmen Conde: Poesía completa*, ed. Emilio Miró (Madrid: Castalia, 2007).
[9] Lynette Roberts, *Collected Poems*, Patrick McGuinness, ed. (Manchester: Carcanet, 2005), pp.41-78,

Spirit put to no better purpose than
Grain of sand. Overwhich. Backwards and
Forwards soldiers ran. Such battles of mule
Stubbornness; or retreat from vast stone walls.

Brought non-existence of past, present and
Future 1, 2, 1, 2, 1, 2, left, right, left, right,
Accumulating into a monotonous pattern
Of dereliction and gloom. When battles should be
Fought at Home: as trencher-companions. *He at my side.*[10]

From her base in Ireland, the last Viscountess Powerscourt, the Hampshire-born, Anglo-Jewish heiress and poet, Sheila Wingfield, née Beddingfield, published her long war poem, *Beat Drum, Beat Heart* in 1946. Currently out of print, it falls into the same category as *Gods with Stainless Ears*.[11] In the first section, 'Men at War', she offers a meditation on the nature of war and the way it corrupts and diminishes all those it does not kill or maim. She gives voice to soldiers from a series of European and Colonial wars, from antiquity to the mid-twentieth century, and allows considerable prominence to the Spanish Civil War, perhaps the last war which saw men, Spaniard and foreigner alike, at least to the untutored eye, rush into battle in defence of an abstract principle only to find it turn to ordure:

Gestures that were heroic are remote
As black clouds in a battle-piece;
They need rain in Barcelona
Where there's blood up to the second storeys.
God of hopes, how you misguide us. We
Who thought we had the heart and sinews
Of strong beasts, of noble birds —
[…]
But see, mine's foul and ragged with deceit
Because, by Ronda bridge across

---

[10] *Gods with Stainless Ears*, Part III, in *Collected Poems*, p. 59.
[11] Sheila Wingfield, *Collected Poems*, (London: Enitharmion, 1983), pp. 19-72.

The double cliffs that sheer to drop eight
Hundred feet, and from whose rocks so many
Pigeons flew, instead, the violated
Nuns fall, fluttering.[12]

In the very last stanza of this first section, Wingfield moves on to establish a compassionate and insightful equivalence between the scars carried by those dispossessed by acts of war, the civilians, and those forever haunted by the acts they carried out in its name, the demobbed and serving soldiers who survived:

By any houseless ones who sit,
Emptied of feeling on a heap of bricks
And grit which was their all;
Chiefly by those who cannot sleep
But — fretting like the wind at night —
Think ceaselessly, had they advanced,
Gone back, been forthright, or declared themselves
Some other time, or place, or way, there would
Have been no utter, endless grief: I swear,
I pray, never again.[13]

Given her Jewish heritage, Wingfield must have felt doubly afflicted by the horrors of Nazi agression in Europe. Nevertheless, she in Wicklow as much as Roberts in Carmarthenshire was at least spared the awfulness of enemy bombardment and occupation, or worse.

One who was spared none of this and whose fiction written under the yoke of Nazi occupation has only of late come, spectacularly, to light is the Russian-born, French novelist of Jewish extraction, Irène Némirovsky. Though she, her husband and children had converted a couple of years earlier to Catholicism, she was arrested by French police as a stateless Jew on July 13th 1942, in Issy l'Évêque, in German-occupied Burgundy. She had moved her two daughters to Issy as the French capital fell in the Summer of 1940 and left Paris definitively for Issy in 1941 when it became

---

[12] *Beat Drum, Beat Heart, Collected Poems*, p. 26.
[13] *Beat Drum, Beat Heart, Collected Poems*, p. 32.

impossible for her husband, like her an emigré Russian Jew, to continue to work as a banker. On July 17th she was transported to Birkenau and she died there on August 17th, probably of typhus, an illness no doubt aggravated by her chronic asthma.[14] Her novel sequence, *Suite française* (French Suite), which she wrote in a white-hot fever of intensity during her time in Issy and the manuscript of which her elder daughter had kept for decades untouched in a trunk, was first published in 2004, to enormous acclaim in France. It was rapidly translated into the major European languages, including into English, a market in which the demand for works in translation is notoriously small.

Némirovsky had been an established novelist in France since the late twenties. She published her first novel *Le Malentendu* (The Misunderstanding) in 1923. Her third, *David Golder*, which appeared in 1929, established her as one of the best-known and most successful novelists of the thirties in France.[15] When *Suite française* came out in October 2004, it was warmly received in the French press. Its success being seen, by many, as a sort of restitution for the betrayal visited on Némirovsky by the adopted homeland which, even though it had denied her the status of citizenship, she refused to desert in its time of need. Clemence Bouloque, for example, argues that in the award of the Prix Renaudot, for the first time posthumously, the jury was perhaps tacitly acting according to 'extra-literary intentions', attempting to institute 'a reparation' and one which might not solely take in Némirovsky, but all those others of her faith and heritage whose lives and wellbeing seemed of such little value to French collaborators.[16] Yet, as Pascal Bruckner points out, Némirovsky, in this sequence of novels on which she was still working on 11th July, two days before her arrest, is intent on looking forwards to a time when all will be well again. Not only that, in Bruckner's analysis,

---

[14] See Olivier Philipponnat and Patrick Lienhardt, *La Vie d'Irène Némirovsky* (Paris: Grasset/Denoël, 2007).

[15] *Le Malentendu* (Paris: Oeuvres libres, 1923); *David Golder* (Paris: Grasset, 1929).

[16] Clémence Boulouque, 'Irène Némirovsky: échec à l'oubli', *Le Figaro*, 9th November 2004. My translation.

she places her trust in the women and children of the Occupied France depicted in the novels:

> Irène Némirovsky combines in a striking manner two elements generally alien to one another: realism and compassion. On the one hand, she adheres to the grand literary tradition from Balzac onwards which depicts man as abased, powerless, and is at heart no more than a novelistic translation of Christian pessimism; on the other, she espouses from the inside the motives, the meanness of her characters, abstains from criticising them. This suspension of judgement, this empathy with human frailty, even more remarkable in a writer living events from day to day and knowing herself to be condemned, is moving: she attenuates the darkness of the narrative, avoids attitudes of indignation or resistantialism. As if the writer wished, from the outset of the conflict, to disarm hatred and prepare a future reconciliation between peoples. Only mothers and carefree young girls arouse her affection. [17]

While this may be rather too black-and-white a judgement on the characters in the novel in general, nonetheless, Bruckner's readiness to allocate importance to the role of women and children in the novel sequence betokens, maybe and quite apart from the agonised complexity of French literary memory of the Capitulation of June 1940, the German Occupation and the Vichy Government, a contemporary literary climate which is prepared to welcome an alternative version of events from the war-torn mid-twentieth century. Certainly, the runaway success of *Suite française* in the English-speaking world and the subsequent interest in the rest of Némirovsky's output attests to the existence of a profound interest in the perspective of women living through war and occupation.

Though Carmen Conde was a much less seasoned writer than her near-contemporary, Némirovsky, when she wrote *Mientras los hombres mueren*, and though dense, modernist prose poetry will

---

[17] Pascal Bruckner, «Elle s'appelait Irène» *Le Nouvel observateur*. 21st October, 2004. My translation.

never have the appeal of a realist, lyrically-phrased sequence of novels, nonetheless, the Spanish Civil War was very much an internationalised, if not strictly speaking, international conflict which would have had an immense impact on the English-speaking world even if it had not been immediately dwarfed by the catastrophe of the Second World War. Carmen Conde's work has been republished and her reputation re-evaluated in Spain as part of the celebration of the centenary of her birth in 2007. There has also been, in Spain, since the Millennium, a process of opening-up with regard to the memory of the Civil War which has seen the enactment of government legislation to recognise the sacrifice and heroism of those on the losing Republican side killed in battle, and executed and imprisoned during and after the war, and which has also witnessed a flowering of prose fiction and memoir exploring the Civil War.[18] The most successful of these works, outside Spain, was Javier Cercas' 2001 novel, *Soldados de Salamina*, translated into English as *Soldiers of Salamis* by Anne McLean in 2003 and made into an internationally distributed film by David Trueba in the same year.[19] In an international, Anglophone context, this fits with the zeitgeist which brought Némirovsky's *Suite française* such signal and immediate success.[20]

It is in this context that I have attempted to produce a translation into English of *Mientras los hombres mueren*. The problems attendant on such a translation project are considerable, the greatest being the difficulty of finding a voice which will work in English for this poetry. Conde's language is at times jagged,

---

[18] The *Ley orgánica de la memoria histórica* (Law of Historical Memory) was approved by the Spanish parliament in November 2007.
[19] Javier Cercas, *Soldados de Salamina* (Barcelona: Tusquets, 2001); *Soldiers of Salamis*, trans. Anne McLean (London: Bloomsbury, 2003); David Trueba, *Soldados de Salamina* (Warner, 2003).
[20] In November 2006, Variety reported that the screenrights to *Suite française* had been bought by Universal Studios. Michael Fleming, 'Checking into 'Suite': Gallic war tale to occupy 'Pianist' scribe', *Variety*, 9th November, 2006.

often obtuse, not always self-explanatory, even to the recondite eye, and at others lyrical and profoundly elegiac.[21]

Translation, is, of course, an arbitrary business and each translator must set his or her own internal parameters. Mine, in practice, have been to attempt to convey as much of the original meaning and imagery in English as I can, to retain as much of the original structure as I can, and to refrain, as far as possible, from embellishments which might make the translation appear more polished in English but which would, of necessity, etiolate the original sequence of images and meanings. I decided to look for a language which retained as far as possible the lyrical possibilities which even prose poetry of this density exudes in a romance language. I might have made a much more radical decision and opted for a much more compacted type of language, closer to English modernist diction. However, as most of the individual poems are expressed in conventional sentence structures, I have retained an equivalent straight-forward non-compacted style, with occasional intensifications of vocabulary, sometimes hyphenated, sometimes not, on the occasions where the poetry demands such compaction.

---

[21] For full analysis in English of the individual poems in the original, see my *Carmen Conde: Mientras los hombres mueren* (Manchester: Manchester University Press, 2009)

While the Men are Dying

While The Men Are Dying was written at a time of intense suffering because of what war was destroying and will continue to destroy. Not just some men in particular, all men are mourned here with the deep sorrow a woman feels when faced with the inscrutable designs which allow horror in where the trusting smile once resided.

The poems, 'To the Children Killed in the War', which figure in this very book, were ripped from my insides in even deeper desperation.

All pain is futile, I knew it then and I know it better now. Yet, even so, saying aloud how much one is suffering because of what cannot be helped seems to melt away all the barriers between ourselves and others.

And that was the only consolation I could find then.

I

While the men are dying, I say unto you, I who sing of desolate provinces of Grief, that sobbing and anguish are breaking in me against ships of furious ebony; and the paired fruit of my lips burns with sighs, for the skies have found themselves pierced by dark curses.

I follow the men who are dying in their search through the muddy roots and seams of soil, for they and I have the same dream design beneath the earth.

Be silent all those who do not feel themselves bent double in agony today, day of shock horror consumed by fire torches of screams, for this woman is telling you that death is in not seeing, nor hearing, nor knowing, nor dying!

II

Can no hand remove the dagger which has multiplied in my heart?... Are those contented with bread, or those wounded by panic, mine? I bring my fingers to the side which was Christ's and I feel the hum of the blood of two thousand years of useless terror.

Who is riding those cold, blue horses which gallop the plateaux where the past raised tragic walls of Avila and Segovia? What warriors' metallic torsos are bathing in the Tagus and the Guadalquivir, along which Athens and Arabia were translated into romance?

The land is fed on fresh seed, for the beings absorbing themselves into it, unfruited, are returning intact the wealth of generations they had no time to propagate.

And my fist-shaped heart, like yours, brothers of the blood in flames, every day finds its geographies of heartbeats more shattered!

III

Into the deepest root of the sea my brothers nailed their screams of terror: we do not want to die! and their eyes made their screams more azure. And the sea carried on growing, mountain after dense mountain of green flesh with collars of winged lace, until the sky received it, taking possession of it amid clamour.

I walked the black nights, with no sun roses on my brow. How could I ignite my brain temples if those I so loved were quenching their embers in the unbridled trembling of death?

Give me, all of you, a boat with the most elegant pavilion of smiles that I may reach the lamentation which swells out of you, Sea, as my own is born in overwhelming agony! For I want to be strong, I want to be agile, I will contain the life which spills itself over the vine of the dead.

IV

The grieving!
The voices come, crying out along avenues of grief sighs.
The grieving!
The mothers come, crying out on startled tenterhooks of lamentation.
The grieving! The grieving! The grieving! I cry out, alone, a river of burnt banks. And there are lights without flames, there is panic in long nails driving into shuddering flesh, beneath my grieving awareness of spirit.

V

DEATH IN THE AIR

Someone told in the ungarrisoned night without angels a rending music of tears. The beings who had already freed themselves from the horror shock of the shrill day of grieving listened with voracious ear and learnt the strict beat of the heart dragging on the pillow.

The one speaking recounted continents and emptied seas; but a simple Spring of leaves, with no risks from feathers, made sharp counterpoint. Those paying attention smiled, fortunate to smell the blue of tender life.

Oh pity the insomniacs no promise, no word will send off to contented sleep!

They will stay fixed, eternal eyes open panic-stricken before the abysses in which the voice of death rolls, coils - a stone with no moss, a river of thorns.

VI

The broken, breathless, shattered land, turned into a prickle of dried-up hearts, a bowl of unopened adolescent gonads. The land blooming with blood, dismembered eyes, squeezed-out breasts. The land holed by screams, by foam, with knees of grief sobbing and death-rattles.

The great land of my father turned to earth!

Running over it, grain by grain, shoeless, thirsty, sticking our lips to the pit of transformed sand which is water, we will hear the dead, the murdered, the suicides, those blown up with dynamite. In the bitter, penetrating darkness of the earth now only Earth.

VII

You males and females laid out in death, stand up only while the ebony steeds of grieving lash this air of Spain with their manes.

Abandon your frenetic beds of lust, males and females who will never be men or women. Endure for a while the spinning in your horizontal heads; let the blood bark in which you will rot know that you are able to walk without rowing along nights of spasm.

World still prostrate, rise up. For pain purifies even those who do not deserve it.

VIII

Which disturbed head dreams and dreams of the same music as mine?... Its dreaming has broken for me the bridges of fine branches along which my sleep used to cross forests and rivers of light!

Which solitary lips kiss themselves?

Which voice speaks tender nothings to itself, remembers or invents impossible dialogues?

What light is there where I am looking for light?

Give me, all of you, dreams of tacit harmonies, eternal repose without forebodings in this present time dramatic consciousness of my life!

IX

    I will certainly never give birth to a child of flesh while the Earth suffers from the yellow furies of War.

    You will not try out your womb while all the terrains along which love moves have their fragrances stilled.

    I will remain, sombre mourning, among the dead who were sons of women who could do nothing against their death.

X

Every day I have a brother fewer on the earth as he adds himself to those who lie among the roots with their foreheads emptied of eyes. Every night sleep hurts me more, for if it entwines me, how can I enjoy it while the men are dying in ocean waves? And I do not sleep, what insanity of nights with the horror present of war!

I am becoming like a tree all of whose branches and leaves are being cut off: my roots in the ground, my brain temples in the air, but with arms for nobody! If I had arms, for whom, if they are all dying?

XI

Mothers!... Or is it the seas crying out in the voice of birth pangs to get death to halt its sowing of hard frosts?

Mothers!... Or is it the olive trees writhing their ardent branch consciousness in an anxiety for light glow without end?

Mothers!... Or is it that those in their last throes have a choir of death-rattles churning green horror shock citrus fruit?

XII

I know well that no selfish ear adapts itself to the spherical light glow exploded from the earth; for this reason their breasts do not resound with terrified voices, growing in horror, rejecting the plural death black rain pours down without ferment for wheat or ferment for silt soil.

Why do you all not listen to what I listen to? I rip apart the night with eyes which tomorrow will be flowers, to gather the sustained splendour of all the eyes which like mine live in the aching darkness. My circulation runs through the same roots as the juices which undermine the earth of the graves; and I live with the blood of candles on my lips, candles the past forgot on impossible cloud altars to gods of tragic destiny, because of these men and these boys splitting apart in an arterial humming beneath the sinister edifices of lamentation!

I know well how alone we are, the dead and I. Even if my brow is of mature sunshine and my hair rises on its roots to the heavens, let nobody ever doubt this anguish in which my body and my soul are dying!

XIII

Those of us from here will never again hear the silence which navigated the nights, nor will the densest night hear its own corporeal bell... How could they soak the cave of freshness from which the nights sprang in so much blood?

Oh, now the woods can no longer be trespassed upon nor birds caught to carry messages to stars!

The cry of thousands of throats, the deep, pealing, tenebrous cry itself, has pierced everything: night, fragrance, and this hollow of a womb which dreamt of being a cradle.

XIV

All the voices came out disbanded; the dust covered, old voices which had been kept in the wineskins of horrifying silence, and the crowds ran mad with lamentation over the darkened flesh of war.

Women whose roots were dry, with others uprooted, with many more invested with grief, cried out to their sons from all the crossroads of wind and terror.

The men who were scattering their bones singing in frenzy deployed their forearms so that the sun eluded light glow.

Only the thoughtful, the mothers, the girlfriends, all the people of bronzed adolescence, inevaporable, could smile in the midst of death.

And I search in my hearing for the germ of a voice which will never go out, which will leap over eternity.

XV

All of you, come to us, the living cynically alive, and drown us in the blood of our bodies despoiled of light glow.

You, the dead in this brutal war of progress, come and strike our alien-to-everything sensibility, forgotten, blooming in its own unique augustness.

We will be terrified that you come deafening the land in uproar, and we will flee without being able to reach life, bricked up by death. Because it is true that while the gunpowder wounds were opening a path for themselves in your bellies, we were all drinking and smiling, fortunate in the also alien sun.

We should disgust ourselves for living longer than you, avenue on avenue, boulevard on boulevard of detonated sons.

XVI

And what can I do for all of you? Tell me.

The Sea gave me his exact order, taking my eyes up into two small, round-keeled boats. The Wind gave me his, taking possession of my hair to spread it out in a blonde kerchief of scent. I received hers from the Earth, growing me up through the columns of my legs, with an inextinguishable and fruit-bearing shudder. All those who command, even Fire, have told me what they require of me!

...And will you say nothing, all of you who are being liquefied by the hurricane of hatred?

For certain I only have one voice, this warmly-veiled voice, with which to try to serve you as intermediary!

XVII

For how many hours can the sinking, splitting step of thousands and thousands of men walking the measureless land of lamentation be heard!

The land shudders, silencing it. The sky tears itself loose, rising above itself. Only the hearts of the longing match their thawing-out to the rhythmic endlessness of the walking.

Where are you going, brothers of the tireless search? What planet of fibres, of viscera, of untouchable and immortal members do you want to find? How my solitary blood listens to you, follows you, for that dreamt-of harmony which none of us will ever hear!

The hermetic steps, exact numbers of the desolate loneliness, open trenches, chasms, gorges,... Could anyone see a sweet-water stream amid the lands opened up by Sorrow..., a shining star in the black skies..., a lit-up, golden smile dawn?

XVIII

The graves began to ache with the groans of the mothers giving birth. Because torn guts were opening up whose fruit it would cost to release into the hand-to-hand with eternity. Who did not have a grave garlanded with shattered hands; who was not bearing roses for the blood spilled in black pools on the asphalt, rose of bomb fires?

Bonfire too of graves in the bankless night of the immense Night of the Grieving of the Spheres! They were all burning, fire torches of the dead green with life, for the unending lamentation of the men to be born.

My brother is become soot beneath the garden in which he painted his first cloud, and my sister weeps for a man above the ground in which I have sunk the feet which sustain my voice.

Who could plunge their avid fingers into the flesh of the land and de-seed it, alien, like dry bread?

XIX

Let nobody speak to me now, as if they loved it, of Eternity! Let nobody come to me with his curse or his ear wounded by hearing what even God himself did not dream of! I have seen buildings fall like burst fruit, the most fragmented voices have collapsed in front of me, beings half in being were left behind on my paths... And they were all eternal, they flowed unceasing from the caves in which Eternity plucked its maddened harps. There my blood learned the brevity of all events.

Because of this pain which I suffer, let nobody come to my tenderness rendered hopeless tears! Well I know that everything is a lie when it comes to Time and the tumescent principle of its eternity... where? in which ambit? Nobody knows where eternal time lives, and the great creature which consumes it as one lover is consumed by another.

Fleeting madness of others coming to my being, describing to me the beautiful perspective of Eternity! I am hearing how, on the earth into which my house is nailed, the thick shrapnel of death falls and falls. I am hearing how those who I love are moving away through where I will never reach their departures. And who will come to tell me about Eternity! I myself, collapsing with lamentation, am as eternal as a breeze! I who see sectioned a world of stone and of flesh. I who achieved the means of stretching out in hope my blood tangled word.

Eternity! I will break open the breast of anybody who comes to mention to me the fabulous dream of my soul in sparks.

XX

Forests of our dead young men! Thickets of the lamentation which shakes its horse manes of cries! With hand on heart you summon me to life.

There is no death, only a profuse avenue of hope! There is no death, even if the young are falling under the big guns' axe blows!

Men do not cause death, men never die owing to themselves. It is senseless death which goes over the hectares of worn-out wombs expunging the memory of their children from them.

And many men go to sleep on the threshold of lamentation; those are the ones who seem dead. But those who pay attention, those who bellow their inflamed zeal for life, are the ones who always move forward, the ones who penetrate the thicknesses of the earth, who spill the morning forth, who triumph, knowing how to die, over death.

XXI

It is the ripe time to weep. Unanimous, all the mothers are wearing their nocturnal mourning ribbons. The bedrooms broke open like rotten fruit, and the young women forgot their breasts. The uproar voice of war arrived.

It is the day to look at the sea without understanding its clockwork movement. It is the time to extinguish lamps and birds. It is the day a perennial lookout rides, clad in mourning.

Squeezed by martyrdom, the mothers look at their bodies, their uninhabited hands and eyes.

XXII

Nobody knows where the light is. And the men go around with their hands outstretched, their brows held high and a hopeful smile on their cold lips. The women await it with their pupils dilated by desire, in any cloud, threshold or isle... I alone am the being who does know her own light!

Can you not see it, you who diligently watch, jumping over me like a current, escaping from my brain temples, hair and shoulders? We will light up the voiceless world of your search!

I am afire, yes: afire with exact midday, with accomplished evening. And my faith in my light is my only light glow.

All of you learn from me how to carry the flame strong and upright.

XXIII

Who believes in me? Who believes in those who are dying? Who believes in the very faith of those who are going to die?

Tremble those of you who live distanced from the immense conflict in which every death is a backward step of life and a winding forward of dreams!

Death in tidal waves cannot be brought about unless the mountains assuage its thickness. Wombs cannot be torn apart unless the air burns death-rattles. No single man dies unless a tragic responsibility grows in those who survive.

Pay attention to the legacy of the dead, cold and distanced men: they are leaving you life, intact vertical life, so that you can definitively proscribe death!

XXIV

The wineskins of shadows were emptied over us. In vain I want to light up. There is so much shadow that the light hunches up and confines itself to my body.

The fields twisted themselves out of their irrigation bells; the planted fields raised up black flowers. Everything journeyed, sombre, along the hills of Dawn and the plains of Night.

My dark pain had three slow wings. Nobody's was the hand which squeezed out black milk for dying flocks. Everybody's were the feet which crunched on strips of ground parched for light.

All of you, see my flame, come to my light glow! I am a cry which fire left among you who hate the Spring, and I will burn until I set your eyes aflame.

XXV

There is solitude in the pain of explosion. Even those who bond together terrified are alone, and those who are alone sway like naked trunks whipped by a typhoon. Nobody is anywhere except within himself in the moment of horror shock.

Only when I used to press close to you, mother, on those immeasurable nights of fear, everyone was united, absolutely all those who love in the world.

Not this early morning of whining detonations, among the shards of which I have raised my voice asking, fruitlessly, for company. My unto-the-moon solitude marks fire letters for me on the walls which shout strident truths at my soul, while the bombs fall rotten, in clusters, all around my anguish.

XXVI

On the day of peace I will feel lost, deafened, dazzled. I will not
know anybody, nor will I have near the one I know today better
than my blood, because peace will dilate all airs and beings will
become lost in them looking for themselves, distancing themselves
from the intimacies which they knotted together in war.

Alone, uninhabited, I will go through peace weeping for it and
weeping for myself, since I forgot tranquillity, security, serenity;
and because, suddenly, planes, cannon fire, cries of horror will
interrupt it for me, I will not know what do to with my liberty (for
whom?) nor my tranquillity...

Let Peace come, let the day of peace arrive for us! Even though
mothers will not recover their dead sons, nor children their fathers,
nor the absent the found again...

XXVII

All of you were coming to me along the ruins of leafy civilisations, through the roots of Herculaneum, Pompeii, Rome... You were coming to me underneath and above the world, and your eyes and your hands brought the smell of petrified flowers.

I was alone, forgotten by you and not knowing anything of myself. When I knew of you, it was first through maps and illustration plates, and that ball crossed with blue threads which are rivers, and burning purples which are seas. Nobody knew of me. In no book, as yet, did the edifice of my intelligence or the high tide of my heart appear. You continued to come; you continued to come all those who had the right to believe yourselves happy because the world hung from your eyes the galleries of its museums, from your arms the rumble of its trains, and from your breasts, torsos, waists, legs, and the light wing of your feet, the shuddering of love. And my voice continued even deeper than all of the roots of all the ruins, than all the pools in which the Greeks and Romans dipped the gold of their statues.

Now, yes, I also go to you through ruins! But my ruins do not have ivy on their walls, nor is there in any of my friezes the interrupted gallop of sculpted victors on their way to Mount Olympus.

XXVIII

Rib to rib, mouth to mouth, body to body, Time and I on this nuptial night of the inauguration of Winter.

War. My blood tightens its necklaces of veins around me. War. Up through my body rise the steps I stopped taking voluntarily. War. I press my hands to my tense, hard and tanned legs. War. War with mud, blood, wings of angels and of doves, Mediterranean cloaks and alleluias of mismatched skies.

Hand in hand, we, Time my lover, carry the orbit of War.

XXIX

If the Wind douses itself in cries of pain and hastens to its own dancing houses, all of you should fear the dead.

Fear the adolescents fallen in the wars without end of the most bellicose men, because the land is full of them and biting winds will grow from them.

Let us fear those who return alive from among the dead. The mutilated. Let the healthy hide themselves, the unscathed, because nobody will pardon their self-satisfaction!

Those who are falling sigh, and the immense sheaf of their breath pushes the Night, greatest ship of mourning, along open streets in my heart.

XXX

We feared Hunger, and we went out into the fields looking for something to pacify it: humble beasts, beings we found who would sacrifice them still to feed our bodies. We returned, in the full roar of warfare, with the things which would light the winter up frugally for us. How many sharp hands awaited, reaching out to our fraternity!

But with us arrived, through the air, death. It threw itself in a wave, provident, as if it were, so very generous, life itself. It fell on the small houses, on the big engines, the miserable carts, and the men who were rushing about at midday, the children crying out at the morning of acid sun, and the women enduring men and children...

Who would eat bread, how much bread would this individual eat if every day death swept through and blew away the hearts of cities? What did hunger matter if death calms all hungers?

And we had an urge to throw the bread, the fruit, the meat we had obtained for the implacable cold onto the debris, seeing those who had merely gone on ahead of us dead like sheep among bits of metal, marble, street cobbles and shrapnel shells.

XXXI

THE HERO

Did one of us split the earth with axe blows? Who knocked down this bark raised up in mountains? What powerful arm wielded the force of God to fight against God and his delirious work?...

There is among us, with me, next to you, a frenetic man spilling himself like a glass of oil, a man in whose eyes everything fits in an impulse and out of whose legs one could make columns for the vault of the heavens. How could the sky dare to fall on the earth if he sinks his head into it to raise it up again, holding it aloft?

We have given birth to a hero, a man who contains in himself, in his imprisoned blood, thousands of beings who died with their madness inside them! Let all those who are not fit to shatter elements be taken from before our wonder-struck eyes!

We are moved by a telluric drunkenness because we find that God himself is a son of ours. The Hero is his essence. The Hero is his science. What does it matter if his heroism is against me or in my favour? What does my death matter if he who kills me is a cyclone, a fury, a volcano, an ocean, a hero!?

I want to die with God. Let it come to me however it comes.

Is there anyone who would want to live amongst weak men, cowards, even if they are brothers? I prefer the hero, whether or not he is my brother! If mine, what a glory of admiration and love; if an enemy, may the fate his clear and true hands bring be good!

A Hero is an envoy of the cosmos. If I am in the right against him and he defeats me, we will recount our conflict to the gods. Now, I am dying for him.

XXXII

The Water will always fall, inextinguishable, joining the lands where today Grieving grazes widely. The Water will not end; it will come out of itself eternal like time in the act. Pure. Infinite presence of the infinite absent God.

Those who suffer will come to the circle of the waters which fall without limit, with their desiccated and snapping thirsts; their mouths of crackling parchment, victims of the Lamentation which was sucking them dry to the point of agony.

It rains on the communities which Death suckles. It rains, and the level of the eyes which look at the rain rises. The buried rock themselves to and fro in the softest of mud, soaked in the eternal water, without end.

XXXIII

Now that the Men have put down their arms, now that they call each other brother and the victors have begun to talk of pardon and forgetting, what do you think, Mother?

Mother, who wear black, up and down the Motherland, what do you feel in your cradle body, in your breasts, dry and burnt by overwhelming anguish?

Mother of the Dead, of the Murdered, of the Fugitives, what do You say?...

WAR IN THE PORT

Gruff, hardened, rhythmic, measured: dockers, undaunted offloaders of watchful, persecuted, now fled ships, undone by the explosive, crackling planes which dupe mirror decoys and loyal cannon vigilance.

Dockers of the port, of which no white stones nor houses raised on feet of fragrant algae remain; who come to offload wheat, sugar, coffee, wool and letters from the absent, and wings for the exalted of the heroic airforce, sails for the humble fishing boats, wheels for the fast cars, fuel for the tyrannical engines... What an inhuman, what a superhuman manhood is yours!

Workers who among sirens, never of song nor music, bring grief to your own houses in order to protect us from hunger; offloaders of indispensable riches condemned to salvo fire, what an unequalled, unprecedented arrogance is yours!

The city runs on along its avenues of fruit, along its canvases of green, to the lordly slenderness of its winged towers; and the sea roars, pants, attracts death, hums, crashes onto the port, where the men are moving their arms with the weight brought by the sea... Heroism of the suffering, of those who are falling after those who have fallen, before those who will fall with their pyramidal Norman horses and their strong carts, among dark metal shards, with brine on their eyes and their lips, like a last baptism!

What man of the city, however timorous, does not feel shame before these dockers? Day by day, backs straight, they cross the grief of rocks and rigging; day by day they fall and fall again among bales; and the marine streets are filled with the blood which lifted barrels, with the teeth which chewed on courage, with the fingers which picked up fear by the scruff of the neck, forcing it to pant in defeat.

Tossed hair, blue eyes, brows into which vigour placed indestructible bones; and the starting passion, the ongoing impulse, the manliness without limits, the physical being brimming over with Cyclopean willpower next to the ships, propitious victims all of the planes which bite, twist men, without lamentation or moaning; they do not fall on excrement when death appears.

Who are the toughest fighting men, working men, but the offloaders of ships, infallibly bombarded?

If it can be done, let the sea be made bigger! Let the sea swell up, let the sailing ships be raised again and the bergantines so they can come into this port!

These Colossi demand a statue of porphyry in the great tower of a free sea.

THERE WAS A WORD

She is already dead, already consumed; a deflowered virgin, a maiden squeezed and worn-out by the grave of unconscious possession.

You will not see her, because she has just fled before my brain temples, full of the mud of her death. In vain will we shout out her trivalent name; her liquid initial, her stem like a round kiss, her clear-cut end, shot report of disorder.

Now you will not see her, you men who ran after her smile. Now you will not see her, you women who felt yourselves saved beneath her gaze.

Did she exist one day amid the confused crowd of shouting, of laughter, of leaps and of assaults? Was her pineal lightning possible when the black horses of routine or permissiveness lay dead?...

If you went after her, to drill through the mountains of cement which separated her! what did you do with her mistreated beauty? What gesture, which brutal word, what greasy and bland lie shocked her agile figure, thickening it, sinking it, ageing it to the point of agony?...

Oh, you men who succumbed and you men who prevailed!... What did all of you do with Liberty?

THE WAR HAS ENDED

The ships' horns have sounded, and in the sombre docks the torrential agonies of thousands of men who wanted to flee, defeated.

The audacious got to a vessel which would save them. But, how many are walking around weeping for their defeat and going on their way in thirst and hunger! Without ready money, without a friendly hand to bring them consolation...

Like a sudden immense avalanche the war ended.

Peace fell in.

To the Children Killed in the War

I

Do not flay them, cannon; do not shred them, machine guns; huge bombs falling from the deep sky who seem to be gifts from the broad clouds, do not shatter the little bodies of the children!

Does the lead not feel pity for these milky-pink shoulders, for these sweet little lifebloods, for these skins like lips? Does no enemy airman have little children who hold up their hands in the propeller downdraft?

No. The enemy does not seem to be a father, and maybe he is an orphan as well. So the children are smashed in smoking craters, and all around the gardens are moss-covered heads of hair, knees in torn silk; scattered amongst the smashed trees, with a sustained grieving of cries which yesterday were kites and today are poor split gums which now will never taste corn cobs nor the fresh nipples of enamoured mothers...

II

The green conch shells of horror shock, and the thundering murmurs of terror, and the viscous long blue finger of fear... Run, children, run along paths clear of gunpowder, as yet without crushed skulls, towards the serene, quiet waters of silence and of life!

Run, little kids pursued by the machine guns' prickles! Leave the men behind, pay no heed to the women, do not listen to any voice other than that of the wind, that of healthy and vital animals; the voice of cosmic continuity, falling into ruin behind your backs, but in itself permanent beyond dying!

Here, death; here blackness; here, war... Run, children, run with your tomorrow!

III

Let the sirens not scream over the tremulous little golden bell ears!

Let all the wings which tear the curved sky of the concave nights be shattered!

Let the cylinders from which hatred is spilled out not end in black mouths!

Has everybody forgotten the cradles, the cradles in which children cry by themselves and sing to themselves?...

IV

The boy was walking along the few little rivulets of a few cold street corners. He carried in his hands, wet with orange juice, a blue cardboard horse...

Who nailed him to the ground with the helix-shaped fuse of the bomb? From which perverse angels were steel knives released?

The horse was safe, warm with clean blood, there was the smoky breath of the plane... Who could look at the street doubled over in horror shock, splitting itself apart in shards of visceral stone beneath the pieces of the bomb-blasted boy!

V

I was aching for a child. All my insides opened up with thirst for a child. Ah, now I know why my vigilant spirit did not want to release a branch!

But I am a mother crucified in all those children who were blown up in sparks at the impetus of hoarse enemy shrapnel. And I am in pain up to where the blood of my womb finishes.

VI

The fruit of your navel was a green cluster which your mother used to kiss, which I used to kiss with new and sweet lips, the laughter of delight opening up with our joy in kissing you.

Now we are both standing beside your death chill. A multiple killing, tangled up in rubble and TNT, has torn you from the life in which we used to lift you up.

Oh, child dead in the flower of sweetness; oh, little boy with your blood spread wide!

VII

The land is feeding itself on little bodies which are weak, but growing and powerful with light, to swell it better than the sun, which could never penetrate it so deep.

Children, war gives children to the dry and harsh dust, bitten into by lilies and butterflies; tender children of the embrace their parents gave each other, shredded beneath the shrapnel like corn cobs de-seeded by an iron hand!

The land sown with unripened generations, what a splendid harvest of guts it will give to the future, brothers racked by war!

VIII

My son lives with me, he goes inside my blood, but I will never give him to all of you if before my body is dry you do not distance war eternally from our soil.

I will not open myself up in fruit so that your fruit can bring death to me.

IX

Let nobody speak to the child to whom death was brought by the hand of man!

Is it possible to dream of love, showing the hand of he who hates?

X

Women who wear mourning because hatred brought death to your laps, refuse to conceive children while men do not erase war from the world!

Refuse to give birth to the man who tomorrow will kill the man who is your sister's son, to the woman who will give birth to another man so he can kill your brother!

XI

If mothers were to hold their children up like fire torches of joy! If those who carried children inside were to point to their wombs where contented lifebloods are moving! If women were to hear the clamour of their guts, they would put an end to wars!

Because all the men who fall down dead, and the women peppered by shrapnel, have given their son, who weeps and bleeds in the war!

XII

Stop, cannon!
Halt, planes, in the middle of your inhospitable sky! Can all of you not hear, machines and men, the immense lamentation of all the orphaned children in the world?

XIII

Water! The Water goes across the fields shouting out: 'Who has seen the dead child, with his marine-blue eyes full of seagulls, and his shoulders become poppies, and his belly opened up like a piece of fruit?'

And the black poplars shout it out, raised up on their shining trunks. The birds shout it out, startled by ravens and eagles.

Because the boy killed by war has given his green voice to those who shout out their lament for him.

XIV

Did you all see the doves stop and hold themselves ecstatic between their wings, in mid-flight?

And did you hear how the rivers raised themselves up onto their knees, lapping at the roots of black trees?

Did you not feel the pain of the wheat, like the scent of warm breasts, in the middle of the bent-double afternoon?

It was because the children were dying under the bombs from the planes, beneath the shells from the big guns of hatred!

XV

Are we going to teach these children who recognise the frightful creaking of houses, who know the noise of bitter explosions on warm and fresh bodies, History? All of you, let them forget this drama; let them learn the tender discourse of animals in Nature; let them stroke flowers and learn from them the treasure of delight that is touch!

Nobody who is conscious would wish to teach History now to childhood. That twisting of human bones, a rattling of teeth, a steaming of lifebloods! And they have seen it with their tiny startled fish little eyes...

No. Let them forget History. Let them play, let them dream. Let nobody mention peoples or men to them. Let everybody point out seas, clouds, plants and animals.

XVI

The children have become so small on the earth strewn with exploded shell casings!... They barely make little wrinkles in the indubitable mosses, little sure insects in the planted fields... Children on the surface? When they cannot be seen from above, from the planes! Children are not seen, ever, from the sky!

And they are here. In myriad. As if the sky, blinded by its star brightness, had emptied its constellations onto the earth. The children are here... Very many, dead now, among the others who sing and dance and wheel their fear in the dark pools of their big eyes... They are here. Will more come?... No, for pity's sake, women! Do not bring forth more children while lightning flashes continue to fulminate against their tender, wheat-ear bodies, their poppy-like, sweet little hearts!

XVII

Streets, bind together! Towers, bend yourselves over the streets! Sea, mountains, move in over the city where the children are playing! There are planes in the sky, there is death in the sky... Stones and branches, waves and woods, move in to guard beneath you the river of delight which flows in the veins of the children!

XVIII

I am afraid. I am afraid of those dry, hole-peppering engines which perforate, which drill the blued, black gold of the night unto its genesis.

I am afraid because I hear the cries of children hurling themselves about in staircases and cellars; their mothers' encouragement; and my hair and my pulses ache hearing death fall as if it were rain searching for tender trees to make them shoot up all of a sudden.

XIX

I want your child, enemy airman; I want your son to show him the destroyed body of mine, so that he can hear you flying, with your bombs and your bullets, over our heads.

Give me your child, you who keep your own in safety. Give him to me, blond and luminous like mine was; I want to see his lips sigh next to my son, in his eyes a weeping in terror of you. Because I am the mother of the one you destroyed and I want you to give me yours intact.

I will not wound him. I will not speak harshly to him. My voice will be pure and valiant in calling him. I only want him to hear you, to know of your raid next to the death of my son!

Give me your son, enemy airman. I will look after him for you, singing to him beside to the grave of mine, dead because of you.

XX

How very many children bleat their tenderness far away, across borders and seas, from our land! To free them from war we condemned them to cold expatriation. To avoid their deaths by metal, we cut them out of our flesh.

They will learn strange things in strange tongues. They will try out their will to love in distant homelands, forever different. They will inaugurate their arms, their conscious thoughts, in countries in which we are strangers.

These children whom the war forces us to save from its brutal impetus cause us pain: by being far away, because they will end up forgetting us, because their homeland will be, in their memory, deep like an arid, wind-blown valley to which they will fear to return, even if the cadavers of their parents await them, their eyes open beneath the skies. To save you, oh, little children! we have reduced ourselves to having no future to hold in our arms.

XXI

Bring back the children!

In the very same warplanes, in the ships which took away and brought in tonnes of lamentation. Bring them back from the distant rains, from the harsh terrains, to their sun and their fruit, to their living mothers and fathers and to their dead.

Bring back to us the children who lost from their mouths the joy of our language. All those we took out amid bombs, sirens, cannon-fire, shocked that in their homeland they must be thrown before death or out abroad. Young mothers of Spain, ask for your children! Do not speak to them of the war. Let them forget (as when they knew nothing in your wombs) how much we wept for them.

Bring us the children, men who have been victorious! We need their torchlight on our brows.